BODY ~~LANGUAGE~~ IN THE WORK PLACE

Body Language in the Work Place

Allan & Barbara Pease

Manjul Publishing House

First published in India by

Manjul Publishing House Pvt. Ltd.

Registered Office:
10 Nishat Colony, Bhopal, INDIA-462 003
Corporate Office:
2nd Floor, Usha Preet Complex,
42 Malviya Nagar, Bhopal, INDIA-462 003
E-mail: manjul@manjulindia.com
Website: www.manjulindia.com

Distribution Office:
SV Book Supply Company Pvt. Ltd.
7/32, Ground Floor, Ansari Road, Daryaganj, New Delhi 110 002
Email: booksupplyco@gmail.com

This edition first published in 2012

ISBN   978-81-8322-247-1

This edition is authorised for sale in the following countries :
India, Pakistan, Bangladesh, Nepal, Bhutan, Myanmar & Sri Lanka

Printed & bound in India by Thomson Press (India) Ltd.

This book is dedicated to all people who have good eyesight but who cannot see.

Contents

Acknowledgements

These are some of the people who have directly or indirectly contributed to this book, whether they knew it or not:

Dr John Tickel, Dr Dennis Waitley, Dr Andre Davril, Professor Phillip Hunsaker, Trevor Dolby, Armin Gontermann, Lothar Menne, Ray & Ruth Pease, Malcolm Edwards, Ian Marshall, Laura Meehan, Ron & Toby Hale, Darryl Whitby, Susan Lamb, Sadaaki Hayashi, Deb Mehrtens, Deb Hinckesman, Doreen Carroll, Steve Wright, Derryn Hinch, Dana Reeves, Ronnie Corbett, Vanessa Feltz, Esther Rantzen, Jonathan Coleman, Trish Goddard, Kerri-Anne Kennerley, Bert Newton, Roger Moore, Lenny Henry, Ray Martin, Mike Walsh, Don Lane, Ian Lesley, Anne Diamond, Gerry & Sherry Meadows, Stan Zermarnik, Darrel Somers, Andres Kepes, Leon Byner, Bob Geldof, Vladimir Putin, Andy McNab, John Howard, Nick & Katherine Greiner, Bryce Courtney, Tony & Cherie Blair, Greg & Kathy Owen, Lindy Chamberlain, Mike Stoller, Gerry & Kathy Bradbeer, Ty & Patti Boyd, Mark Victor Hansen, Brian Tracy, Kerry Packer, Ian Botham, Helen Richards, Tony Greig, Simon Townsend, Diana Spencer, Princes William and Harry, Prince Charles, Dr Desmond Morris, Princess Anne, David & Jan Goodwin, Iven Frangi, Victoria Singer, John Nevin, Richard Otton, Raoul Boielle, Matthew Braund, Doug Constable, George Deveraux, Rob Edmonds, Gerry Hatton, John Hepworth, Bob Heussler, Gay Huber, Ian McKillop, Delia Mills, Pamela Anderson, Wayne Mugridge, Peter Opie, David Rose, Alan White, Rob Winch, Ron Tacchi, Barry Markoff, Christine Maher, Sallie & Geoff Burch, John Fenton, Norman & Glenda Leonard

and

Dorie Simmonds, whose encouragement and enthusiasm drove us to write this book.

Introduction

As a young boy, I was always aware that what people said was not necessarily what they meant or were feeling and that it was possible to get others to do what I wanted if I read their real feelings and responded appropriately to their needs. At the age of 11, I began my sales career selling rubber sponges door-to-door after school to make pocket money and quickly worked out how to tell if someone was likely to buy from me or not. When I knocked on a door, if someone told me to go away but their hands were open and they showed their palms, I knew it was safe to persist with my presentation because, despite how dismissive they may have sounded, they weren't aggressive. If someone told me to go away in a soft voice but used a pointed finger or closed hand, I knew it was time to leave. I loved being a salesperson and was excellent at it. As a teenager, I became a pots and pans salesman, selling at night, and my ability to read people earned me enough money to buy my first property. Selling gave me the opportunity to meet people and study them at close range and to evaluate whether they would buy or not simply by watching their body language.

At the age of 20 I became a life insurance salesman for the largest company in Australia and, after becoming the youngest person to sell over a million dollars worth of business in their first year, went on to break several sales records. This achievement qualified me for the prestigious Million-Dollar Round Table in the US and later to be made a fellow. The techniques I'd learned as a boy when reading body language while selling pots and pans could be transferred to other areas of sales. Armed with these skills, I realised I could make a success of almost any business venture.

ALLAN PEASE

The ability to read and decode body language is undoubtedly the best qualification for a successful career.

In this book we'll share with you the techniques we developed for success in sales and business, and will teach you the body-language 'vocabulary' Allan and I have accumulated over our highly rewarding careers. Fundamentally, over the years the work place has changed little, but the introduction of modern technology, such as conference-calling, BlackBerries, iPhones, email and laptops, and the increasingly global nature of business, have created new challenges as well as new opportunities for the 21st-century businessperson. *Body Language in the Work Place* includes plenty of up-to-the-minute tips that will put you ahead of the game. This book will make you more aware of your own non-verbal cues and signals, and will show you how to use them to communicate effectively with coworkers and business associates, enabling you to get the reactions you want in any professional encounter.

At times, the modern work place can seem like a minefield, a dark room in which you fumble around. This book will be like turning on the lights to see what was always there, but now you'll know exactly how things are, and what to do about them. Armed with the information in this book, we hope work becomes a pleasure as you climb the career ladder, and negotiate any obstacles, with ease.

BARBARA PEASE

Body Language
in the Work Place

Interviews:
How to Get the Job . . .
Every Time

Adam left the interview suspecting he'd done badly.

Was it what he'd said that blew it? Or perhaps his chocolate-brown suit, goatee beard, tattoo, earring and overstuffed briefcase had turned them off?

Or had he simply sat in the wrong chair?

First impressions always come first

Most job interviews are non-productive because studies show a strong correlation between how much the interviewer likes the interviewee and whether or not they get the job. In the end, most of the factual information that comes from the curriculum vitae – the real stuff about the candidate that is a good indicator of performance – is forgotten. What is remembered is the impression the candidate made on the interviewer.

> First impressions are the 'love-at-first-sight' of the business world.

What's more, research shows that the first *15 seconds* of an interview are vital – proof that you really don't get a second chance to make a first impression. Other people will form up to 90% of their opinion about you in the first 4 minutes, and 60–80% of the impact you make will be non-verbal. Your approach, handshake and overall body language will largely decide the outcome of your interview. If you want to be a first-rate interviewee, remember to put first impressions first.

Gesture less to be an interview success

High-status individuals use fewer gestures than low-status individuals – people with power don't have to move much. People who are cool, calm, collected and in control of their emotions use clear, deliberate movements. If you want to make a good impression, you should use minimal body movement.

> James Bond is so cool he can even make love immediately after killing ten villains . . . and you can guarantee he'd never fail a job interview.

Special Agent James Bond uses these principles to great effect. When he is being intimidated by baddies, being insulted or shot at, he remains relatively motionless and speaks in short, colourful sentences. Actors such as Jim Carrey are the opposite – they often play highly animated roles, emphasising a lack of power, and usually play powerless, intimidated men. If you had to interview James Bond or Jim Carrey for an executive position, which one would get the job? When it comes to gestures in interviews, less is definitely more.

Body Language at Work

Always carry a briefcase or laptop bag to one side when you go for an interview or meeting, preferably in your left hand, which allows you to shake hands smoothly with your right hand without fumbling. If you're a woman, never carry a briefcase or laptop bag and a handbag at the same time – you will be perceived as less businesslike and more disorganised. And never use any bag as a barrier between you and another person. It conveys insecurity and anxiety, as it demonstrates that you are trying to protect your body and disguise nervousness. Show your confidence by making your body language open.

Body Language at Work   Rule No. 2

Respect the other person's personal space, which will be largest in the opening minutes of the interview. If you move too close, the interviewer may respond by sitting back, leaning away or using repetitive gestures such as drumming the fingers.

Fiddling with jewellery, watches, mobile phones and cufflinks are all interviewing no-nos. The Cuff-Link-Adjust is the trademark of Prince Charles, and is a favourite of the insecure and anxious.

The five things you should *never* do in an interview

1. **Don't wear a goatee to an interview** (especially if you're a woman). While it may be a fashion statement, it subconsciously repels older people because of its subliminal association with Satan caricatures. In Hollywood movies, the villains wear goatees because they are sinister.

2. **Never overfill your briefcase or folder.** It will make you look disorganised.

3. **Never sit on a low sofa** that sinks so low it makes you look like a giant pair of legs topped by a small head – if necessary, sit upright on the edge so you can control your body language and gestures.

4. **Avoid talking for long periods.** High-status individuals communicate effectively in short, clear sentences, so don't talk endlessly. This is particularly important in a phone interview as all the interviewer has to judge you on is what you're saying.

5. **Never shake hands directly across a desk.** Step to the left of a rectangular desk as you approach to avoid being given a Palm-Down handshake, which would immediately put you in a 'one-down' position.

'I hope I haven't talked too much!'

The five things you should *always* do in an interview

1. **Walk into your interview with confidence.** Your entry tells others how you expect to be treated. Don't stand in the doorway like a naughty child waiting to see the headmaster! Even if your interviewer is on the phone, walk in briskly with a smooth motion, put down your briefcase, laptop bag or folder, shake hands and sit down immediately.

2. **Use the interviewer's name** twice in the first 15 seconds. Not only does it make that person feel important, you will remember their name through repetition.

3. **Angle your chair, or body, 45 degrees away from the interviewer.** This prevents you being stuck in the face-to-face 'reprimand' position and takes the pressure off your interview.

4. **Use power words, particularly in phone interviews.** Research shows that some of the most persuasive words are 'discovery', 'guarantee', 'love', 'health', 'money', 'easy' and 'you'.

5. **Plan your exit** – pack your things calmly and deliberately, not in a frenzy, shake hands, turn and walk out. If the door was closed when you entered, close it when you leave. If you are female, always turn back to face the interviewer and smile. The last thing you want them to remember is your face, not your rear end.

BODY LANGUAGE AT WORK FOR HER

In interviews, and at work, women should wear pale or muted lipstick. Research demonstrates that women who wear no lipstick at all in business are seen as more serious about work than men but lacking in personal skills, while women with muted or pastel colours are seen as career-oriented and businesslike. A woman should only wear bright red lipstick if she is interviewing for a profession that promotes female image and attractiveness, such as clothing, cosmetics, hairdressing or pole-dancing.

BODY LANGUAGE AT WORK FOR HIM

Men should never wear a chocolate-coloured suit if their interviewer is female – research shows that women find them a turn-off. Historically, brown clothing has been the colour of animal furs and in later times was the badge of lower-status males. Women look at a male candidate's hair length, clothes design and coordination, the creases in his trousers and shine on his shoes. Most men are completely unaware that women look at the condition of the backs of their shoes as they walk out and mark them down on appearance. If you are male, polish your whole shoe, not just the front.

The best-kept secret of the successful interviewee

Many people are taught that you should maintain strong eye contact with the interviewer until you are seated. This creates problems for both parties. A man wants to check out a woman's hair, legs, body shape and overall presentation. If she maintains eye contact, it restricts this process, so he's left trying to steal glances at her during the interview without getting caught and so becomes distracted from the actual job of interviewing. Some women are disappointed that, in the supposedly equal 21st century, men still do this, but hidden cameras show this to be a fact of business life. Women interviewers go through the same evaluation process with both male and female interviewees, but their wider peripheral vision means they rarely get caught doing it.

Like it or not, every interviewer steals a look at a woman's rear when she leaves a room, even if they don't like her front view.

The secret is, when you go for an interview, shake hands and then give the interviewer a two- to three-second frame of uninterrupted time for them to complete the process of looking you over. Look down to open your briefcase or folder, or to arrange any papers you might need, switch off your BlackBerry or iPhone, turn to hang up your coat or move your chair in closer, and then look up.

Are You Sitting Comfortably? How to Sit, Where and Why

'Just feel at home and tell me all about it!'

It's not what you say, it's where you sit

Here's the lowdown on the common seating plans used by today's business executives:

1. **The rectangular desk,** which is usually the work desk, is used for business activity, brief conversations, reprimands and so on. It lets everyone take a 'position' on a subject and encourages direct eye contact.

2. **The round table,** often a coffee table with wraparound seating or lower chairs, is used to create an informal, relaxed atmosphere or to persuade. King Arthur used this to give his knights equal authority. Theoretically, everyone is equal, but in practice, if someone at the table is higher status than the others, it alters the power distribution. The nearer you sit to the king, the more power you have.

3. **Square tables** create cooperation from the person beside you but resistance from those opposite, and when four people are seated, everyone has someone sitting opposite them. Square tables belong in canteens.

Where you sit in a business situation says a great deal about your status and can greatly influence your relationships with your coworkers. People who are engaged in friendly, cooperative conversation will sit next to each other or on either side of a corner of a table, whereas those engaged in confrontation will sit opposite one another.

And it's not just where you sit, it's what you're sitting on

Have you ever been for a business meeting and felt overwhelmed or helpless when you sat in the visitor's chair? It is likely that the other person had cunningly arranged their office to raise their own status and power, and lower yours. Here's what to watch out for:

1. **Size and accessories.** The height of the back of the chair raises or lowers a person's status. The higher it is, the more power and status the person is perceived to have. How much power would the Queen or the Pope have if they were always sitting on a small piano stool? Swivel chairs have more power and status than fixed chairs, allowing the user freedom of movement when under pressure.

2. **Height.** Status is gained if your chair is higher from the floor than the other person's. Some advertising executives are known for sitting on high-backed chairs that are adjusted for maximum height, while their visitors sit opposite, in the defensive position or on a sofa or chair that is so low their eyes are level with the executive's desk.

3. **Location.** Most power is exerted on a visitor when their chair is placed directly opposite. A common power-play is to place the visitor's chair as far away as possible from the executive's desk, further reducing the visitor's status.

Avoid being stuck in any physical position that takes away your confidence or presence.

Body Language at Work   **Rule No. 3**

A boss should never sit directly opposite an employee if they want to be liked – this position makes two people more likely to argue, feel less at ease and be less able to recall what is being said. Sitting directly opposite others creates bad vibes. This position should only ever be used if you want to reprimand someone or feel superior.

Body Language at Work

Rule No. 4

Studies show that school pupils perform better when seated on the teacher's left, as teachers focus more of their attention on the left of the class than the right. If you're a salesperson, sit the customer on your left to make more business deals. In meetings, however, be sure to sit to the right of the boss for extra perceived power.

BODY LANGUAGE AT WORK FOR HER

If you are a woman, avoid crossing your legs when you're sitting with businessmen unless you are wearing a long A-line dress or skirt, or at least one that is below the knee-line. Even in today's world, the sight of a woman's thighs is distracting to almost all men and detracts from her message. They'll remember who she was but won't remember much of what she said. The same is seen in the media: over 90% of female television hosts are presented with short dresses and exposed legs. This is because studies prove that male viewers will watch the programme for longer, but the same studies also show that the more leg a woman shows, the less men can remember what she has said. The rule here is simple – for social contexts, exposed crossed legs are fine, but don't do it in business.

Women who show high feminine signals in a serious business meeting lose credibility.

BODY LANGUAGE AT WORK FOR HIM

If you're a man dealing with women in business, keep your knees together. The **Legs-Spread** gesture is almost exclusively a male gesture and is also seen among apes who are trying to establish authority over other apes. Rather than risk injury fighting, they spread their legs and the ape with the biggest display is seen as the most dominant. With male humans, even though it's usually done unconsciously, it sends a powerful message. It has very negative effects when a man uses it in front of women during business meetings. Many women respond by crossing their legs and arms, which immediately puts them on the defensive, or they become aggressive without knowing why they feel that way.

Tip: If you're a woman who is constantly confronted by crotch-displaying males, don't react when they do it. It can work against you only if you respond defensively. Instead, try talking to his crotch – responses such as 'You've got a good point there, Bob' and 'I can see where you're coming from' can teach a valuable lesson as well as causing riotous laughter when used at the right time.

The evolution of modern businessman

Sit at an angle to build relationships . . .

Sitting at 45 degrees gives an informal, relaxed attitude to the meeting. It's a great position to find yourself in at your annual job appraisal.

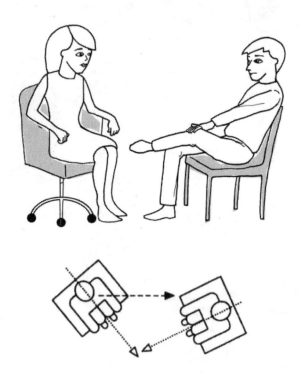

Opening a session using a 45-degree angle keeps things relaxed

You can show non-verbal agreement with a subordinate from this position by mirroring their movements and gestures. When you position your body 45 degrees away from the other person, you take the pressure off the inter-view. This is an excellent position from which to ask delicate or embarrassing questions, encouraging more open answers to your questions without the other person feeling as if they are being pressured.

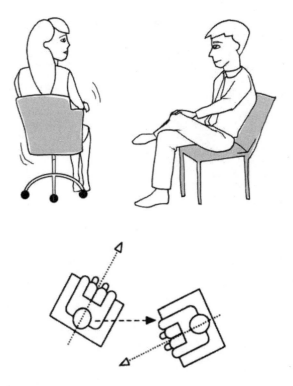

The Right 45-Degrees-Away position

. . . and sit competitors with their backs to the door

Studies reveal that when our backs are towards an open space we become stressed, blood pressure increases, our heart beats faster, our brainwave output increases and we breathe more quickly as our body readies itself for a possible rear attack. This is an excellent position in which to place your opponents.

The two sitting positions men should never use at work . . . and how to deal with them

Centuries ago, men used shields to protect themselves from the enemy; today, civilised man uses whatever he has at his disposal when he is under physical or verbal attack. This includes standing behind a desk or **Straddling-a-Chair**.

The back of the chair acts as a shield and can transform a person into an aggressive personality. Most Straddlers are dominant types who will try to take control of others when they become bored with the conversation, and the back of the chair serves as good protection from any 'attack' by other members of the group.

The Straddler wants to dominate or control
while, at the same time, protecting his front

Tip: The easiest way to disarm the Straddler is to stand up or sit behind him, making him feel vulnerable to attack and forcing him to change his position. This can work well in a group situation because the Straddler will have his back exposed and is compelled to change position. Alternatively, conduct your conversation standing up, looking down on the Straddler, and move into his personal space. This is unnerving for him and he can even fall backwards off his chair in an attempt to move away.

The Catapult: cool, confident, knows it all and thinks he has more bananas than you.

The Catapult is almost entirely a male gesture used to intimidate others or infer a relaxed attitude to lull you into a false sense of security just before he ambushes you. It's commonly used by chimpanzees, and is typical of accountants, lawyers, sales managers or people who are feeling superior, dominant or confident about something. If we could read this person's mind, he would be saying, 'I have all the answers,' or even, 'Maybe one day you'll be as smart as me.' Women quickly develop a dislike for men who use the Catapult in business meetings.

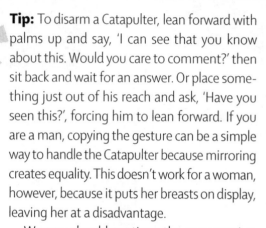

Tip: To disarm a Catapulter, lean forward with palms up and say, 'I can see that you know about this. Would you care to comment?' then sit back and wait for an answer. Or place something just out of his reach and ask, 'Have you seen this?', forcing him to lean forward. If you are a man, copying the gesture can be a simple way to handle the Catapulter because mirroring creates equality. This doesn't work for a woman, however, because it puts her breasts on display, leaving her at a disadvantage.

Women should continue the conversation standing up. This forces the Catapulter to change position. When he stops the Catapult, sit down again. If he catapults again, stand up. This is a non-aggressive way of training others not to try to intimidate you. On the other hand, if the person using the Catapult is your superior and is reprimanding you, you will intimidate him by copying this gesture. Take note if you value your job!

Even flat-chested women who attempt the Catapult are described as aggressive by both men and women.

Seating in the modern office

Open-plan seating is the norm in most offices, with the exception of very high-ranking individuals. So how can you give yourself a status boost if your office is designed for equality? First and foremost, ensure your work space is tidy and professional-looking. Keep photos, ornaments and other personal touches for the home. And to give yourself a real credibility boost, at your next health-and-safety assessment ensure you are given a chair with armrests, wheels and that allows you to lean back: research shows that these components give you more perceived power.

How to Take Your Career in Your Hands:
the Art of Handshaking, Networking and Surviving the Office Party

'You're a memorable person . . . whoever you are.'

It was Adam's first day on the job with his new PR company and he wanted to make a good impression on everyone. As he was introduced to colleague after colleague, he shook their hands enthusiastically and gave everyone a broad smile. Adam stood 6 feet 3 inches tall and was handsome, well dressed and certainly looked like a successful PR man. He always gave a firm handshake, just the way his father had taught him when he was young. So firm, in fact, that it drew blood on the ring fingers of two female colleagues and left several others feeling injured. Other men competed with Adam's handshake – that's what men do. The women, however, suffered in silence and soon were whispering, 'Stay away from that new guy, Adam – he's a bruiser!' The men never brought it up, but the women simply avoided Adam. And half the firm's bosses were women.

Why the power is in your hands

Shaking hands is a relic of our ancient past. Whenever primitive tribes met under friendly conditions, they would hold their arms out with their palms exposed to show that no weapons were being held or concealed. Although humans have been shaking hands for millennia, many of us still haven't mastered the art. The fact is, few people really consider how their hands behave or the way they shake hands when they meet someone, yet those first five to seven pumps establish whether dominance, submission or power-plays will take place. Get it right and you'll make a great impression or seal a business deal; get it wrong and you'll have colleagues talking about you behind your back and clients running for the door.

> A good handshake can be the difference between a career boost and career suicide.

Establishing who has the upper hand

Throughout history an open palm has been associated with truth, honesty, allegiance and submission. Many oaths are still taken with the palm of the hand over the heart, and the palm is held in the air when somebody is giving evidence in court. The palm facing up is used as a submissive, non-threatening gesture, reminiscent of the street beggar, whereas if your palm is turned to face downwards, you will project immediate authority.

When you shake someone's hand for the first time, the position of your palms will have a dramatic bearing on the outcome of the meeting. In Roman times two leaders would meet and greet each other with what amounted to a standing version of modern arm-wrestling. If one leader was stronger than the other, his hand would finish above the other's hand in what became known as the Upper-Hand position.

When shaking hands, one of three basic attitudes is subconsciously transmitted:

1. **Dominance:** 'This person is trying to dominate me. I'd better be cautious.'

2. **Submission:** 'I can dominate this person. They'll do what I want.'

3. **Equality:** 'I feel comfortable with this person.'

These attitudes are sent and received without our being aware of them, but, with a little practice and application, they can dramatically influence any face-to-face meeting.

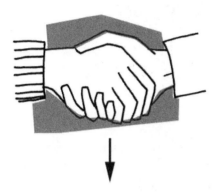

This person means business

Dominance is transmitted by turning your hand (striped sleeve) so that your palm faces down in the handshake. Your palm doesn't have to face directly down, but is the upper hand and communicates that you want to take control of the encounter.

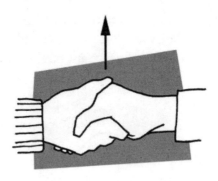

The submissive handshake

The opposite of the dominant handshake is to offer your hand (striped sleeve) with your palm facing upwards. This can be effective if you want to give the other person control or allow them to feel that they are in charge of the situation – if, for example, you were making an apology to a business contact.

To create rapport in a handshake, keep your palm vertical and give the same hand pressure the other person gives you.

BODY LANGUAGE AT WORK FOR HER

> **Women who initiate a firm handshake are rated – in most countries – as more open-minded and make better first impressions.**

Women can tend to give men soft handshakes that convey submissiveness. This is a way of highlighting their femininity or implying that domination of her may be possible. In a business context, this approach can be disastrous for a woman because men will give attention to her feminine qualities and ignore her professional skills. Women who display high femininity in business settings are not taken seriously by other businessmen or other women, despite the fact that it's now fashionable or politically correct to say everyone is the same. One study at the University of Alabama also found that women who are open to new ideas use firm handshakes. Men use the same handshakes whether they are open to new ideas or not. So it makes good business sense for women to practise firmer handshaking, particularly with men.

> **Our study of senior management executives revealed that 88% of males and just 31% of females use the dominant Upper-Hand ritual.**

BODY LANGUAGE AT WORK FOR HIM

The average male hand can exert around twice the power of the average female hand, so it's little wonder that women frequently complain that men grip too tightly in handshakes. Men should make allowances for this. Evolution has allowed male hands to exert a grip of up to 100 pounds for actions such as tearing, gripping, carrying, throwing and hammering. In business, though, a handshake doesn't need to crush bones! The best advice is to practise your handshake on friends and relatives, and to ask for feedback.

The top three handshake tips for disarming a power-player . . .

If you feel a business associate is giving you an overbearing, dominant handshake, forcing your hand down into a submissive position, there are several ways you can counter it:

1. **The Hand-on-Top technique.** Shake hands with the right and then put your left hand over their right to form a **Double-Hander** and straighten the handshake. This is particularly good for a woman to use on an aggressive man, as it switches the power from him to her.

The Double-Hander

2. **Left Foot Forward.** Most people step into a handshake on their right foot. Practise stepping forwards with your left foot, so you're stepping across the other person, making it easier to deal with controlling power-players.

3. **The Last Resort.** If you feel a power-player is purposefully and repeatedly trying to intimidate you, grasp their hand on top and shake it. This can shock a power-player, so you need to be very selective when using it.

The Last Resort

. . . and for creating rapport

A great handshake will convey a feeling of equality and mutual respect. This is the best possible opener for a work-place encounter. Here's how to achieve it:

1. **Vertical position.** Make sure that yours and the other person's palms are in the vertical position so that no one is dominant or submissive.

2. **Match pressure.** You should apply the same pressure you receive. This means that if, on a firmness scale of 1–10, your handshake registers a 7 but the other person is only a 5, you'll need to back off 20% in strength. If their grip is a 9 and yours is a 7, you'll need to increase your grip by 20%.

3. **Convey sincerity.** The handshake evolved as a gesture to say hello or goodbye or to seal an agreement, so it always needs to be warm, friendly and positive.

Tip: If you are meeting a group of ten people, for instance at a networking event, you'll probably need to make several adjustments of angle and intensity to create a feeling of rapport with everyone and to stay on an equal footing with each person.

Use this handshake-horror at your peril . . .

The Wet Fish. Few business greetings are as uninviting as the Wet Fish, particularly when the hand is cold or clammy. A limp, weak handshake is universally unpopular and associated with a weak character, and is a dead giveaway of the nervous businessperson.

Tip: Keep a handkerchief in a pocket or handbag so that you can dry your palms immediately before a business meeting so you don't make a poor first impression. Alternatively, before a meeting, simply visualise that you are holding your palms in front of an open fire. This visualisation technique is proven to raise the temperature of the average person's palm by 3–4 degrees.

. . . and avoid this career catastrophe if you value your job

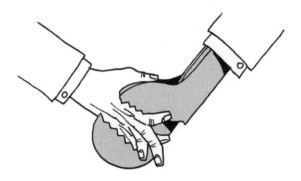

The Bone-Crusher is the most feared of all handshakes as it leaves an indelible memory on the recipient's mind and fingers, and impresses no one other than the initiator. The Bone-Crusher is the trademark of the overly aggressive personality who, without warning, seizes the early advantage and attempts to demoralise his opponent by grinding their knuckles to a smooth paste. If you are female, avoid wearing rings on your right hand in business encounters, as the Bone-Crusher can draw blood and leave you to open your business dealings in a state of shock.

Tip: Though there are no effective ways to counter the Bone-Crusher, if you believe someone has done it on purpose, you could bring it to everyone's attention by saying, 'Ouch! That really hurt my hand. Your grip is too strong.' This puts the advocate of the Bone-Crusher on notice not to repeat the behaviour.

Networking by numbers

Never have your relationships with colleagues, clients and business acquaintances been more important than in today's work place. In fact, truly savvy employees understand that your business relationships are every bit as important as how well you do your job, if not more so. In short, it's not what you know, it's *who* you know. Presenting yourself as a professional, likeable and confident person at conferences, work parties, team-building days, business trips, networking events and after-work drinks can seal a deal, get that promotion and even put you in line for an advantageous move or career change. Harness the power of business-networking websites, such as LinkedIn, and follow our top tips for networking:

1. Stand at 45 degrees to a new business associate you want to feel comfortable around you. This creates openness and also leaves space for a third person to enter the conversation.

2. If you wish to have a more private conversation with someone, or really want to get their attention, stand directly facing the other person, rather than angled away. If you're a woman, however, beware of doing this to a man, as you risk him thinking you are making a sexual advance.

The Open Triangular Position encourages the entry of a third person

3. Act confidently and people will assume you are a confident, capable person. Practise open, approachable body
   language and you'll soon find people are swapping business cards with you.

4. If you are going over to speak to someone at a networking event, never approach them from behind if they are
   female (research shows that women fear attack from
   behind), and never approach from the front if they are
   male (as men fear frontal attack).

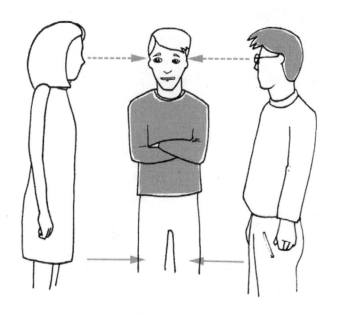

Time to leave this conversation if you want to avoid
a networking no-no

5. Read body-language cues before entering an existing conversation, even if you know the people involved. The **Open Triangular Position** invites you in, but the **Closed Position** will mean you're not welcome.

Body Language at Work

At a networking event lightly touching a person's elbow with your left hand while shaking hands with your right can create a powerful result. Touch creates a momentary bond between two people and leaves a memorable impression. For this to be effective, ensure you touch directly on the elbow, not above or below. Also, ensure you touch for under three seconds, as touching for longer receives a negative response, with the person suddenly looking down at your hand to see what you are doing. When meeting a new business contact, you could also try repeating their name to confirm you heard it correctly and watch their reaction. Not only does it make that person feel important, it helps you remember their name.

> **Touching – when done discreetly – grabs attention, reinforces a comment, increases your influence over others and creates positive impressions on everyone.**

Body Language at Work

Although it is a generally accepted custom in business to shake hands when meeting a person for the first time, it may not always be appropriate for you to initiate a handshake. If you are meeting people at a work party or more informal business event, be sure to ask yourself whether a handshake is appropriate before initiating. You don't want to risk looking overly formal or outdated if the event is more casual. Sometimes a simple head nod is more acceptable.

If you are visiting a foreign country, first check what the local greeting signals are that are used there.

Avoiding the perils of the office party

The office party may seem like a social occasion when you can let your hair down, but it contains many pitfalls for the uninitiated:

1. **Drink only in moderation.** While it might be tempting to treat a work function as you would a night out with friends, remember that this is still a business setting and you will be judged on your behaviour. We all know people who got drunk at the office party, said something offensive or flirted with their boss. Don't let yourself be that person. And whatever you do, steer clear of the photocopier!

2. **Avoid smiling too much at male colleagues if you're female.** Research shows that men tend to mistake friendliness and smiling for sexual interest. This is because men see the world in more sexual terms than women; men have 10 to 20 times more testosterone than women, which makes them view the world in terms of sex.

3. **Women should avoid body language that highlights their femininity** – fondling the stem of a wine glass, hair-flicking and so on – if they want to be taken seriously in the work place, including at office parties.

4. **If you are in a relationship with someone at work,** avoid public displays of affection, even at work parties and functions. Keep your relationship strictly separate from work.

Boosting your popularity with work colleagues

The next time you attend a work function or nip out with colleagues for a drink after work, notice the number of people who have taken the identical gestures and posture of the person with whom they're talking. Mirroring is the way one person tells another that they are in agreement with their ideas and attitudes. One is non-verbally saying to the other, 'As you can see, I feel the same as you.' Take, for example, the two men standing at the bar in the illustration below . They are mirroring, so it's reasonable to assume that they are discussing a topic on which they have similar thoughts and feelings. If one man uses an evaluation gesture or stands on the other foot, the other will copy. One puts a hand in his pocket, the other copies again.

Mirroring happens among friends or between people of the same status, so this means that mirroring colleagues or business associates in an informal business context, such as an office party or networking function, can be a powerful way of building relationships and creating rapport.

Tip: Spend a little time chatting to people around the water-cooler, photocopier or in the office kitchen and you'll build rapport as well as be kept in the loop with office gossip. Just don't spend too long there or you risk being thought of as a time-waster.

When businessmen and businesswomen shake hands

> Business meetings between men and women can be thrown off course by poor handshake technique.

Although women have had a strong presence in the workforce for several decades, many men and women still experience degrees of fumbling and embarrassment in male–female greetings. Most men report that they received some basic handshaking training from their fathers as boys, but few women report the same. As adults, this can create uncomfortable situations when a man reaches first to shake a woman's hand but she doesn't see it. Feeling awkward, the man pulls his hand back, but as he does, she reaches for it and is also left with her hand dangling in a void. He reaches for her hand again, resulting in a mish-mash of tangled fingers that feel like two eager squid in a love embrace.

Tip: If you get caught in a handshake fumble, take the other person's right hand in your left, place it correctly in your right hand and say with a smile, 'Let's try that again!' This can give you an enormous credibility boost with the other person because it shows you care enough about meeting them to get the handshake right. A wise strategy for women in business is to present your hand as early as possible to give notice of your intention. This will avoid any fumbling.

Persuasive Presentations

─── ─── ─── ─── ─── ─── ─── ─── ─── ─── ───

'Do you talk in your sleep?' he asked the speaker.
'No,' came the reply.
'Then please don't talk in mine.'

─── ─── ─── ─── ─── ─── ─── ─── ─── ─── ───

Get on the right side of your audience . . . or the left

> *The Book of Lists* – an annual volume that lists all sorts of information about human behaviour – shows public speaking as our number-one fear, with fear of death ranking, on average, at number seven. Does this mean that people would rather die than deliver a presentation at work?

If you are asked to address a group of people at work, it's important to understand how an audience receives and retains information. When you stand to the audience's left – the right side of the stage – your information will have a stronger effect on the right brain hemisphere of your audience's brain, which is the emotional side in most people. Standing to the audience's right – the left side of stage – impacts the audience's left brain hemisphere. This is why an audience will laugh more and laugh longer when you use humour and stand to the left side of the stage, and why they respond better to emotional pleas and stories when you deliver them from the right side of the stage. Comedians have known this for decades – make them laugh from the left and cry from the right. Use this strategy in your business presentations and you'll be sure to get on the right side of your audience.

Pay attention to who sits where

Studies show that people who sit in the front row learn and retain more than others in the audience, partially because those in the front row are keener to learn, and they show more attention to the speaker in order to avoid being picked on. Those in the middle sections are the next most attentive and ask the most questions, as the middle section is considered a safe area, surrounded by others. The side areas and back are the least responsive and attentive.

In one experiment we conducted, we placed name cards on delegates' seats so they could not take their usual positions. We intentionally sat enthusiastic people to the sides and rear of the room and well-known back-row hermits sat in the front. We found that this strategy not only increased the participation and recall of the normally negative delegates who sat up front, it also decreased the participation and recall of the usually positive delegates who had been relegated to the back.

Tip: If you are giving a business presentation and really want someone to get the message, put them in the front row. Some presenters have abandoned the 'classroom-style' meeting concept for smaller groups and replaced it with the 'horseshoe' or 'open-square' arrangement because evidence suggests that this produces more participation and better recall as a result of the increased eye contact between all attendees and the speaker. With the 'horseshoe position', everyone is sitting in the front.

The power of PowerPoint

Research shows that of the information relayed to the brain in visual presentations, 83% comes via the eyes, 11% via the ears and 6% through the other senses, so if you are going to use visual aids, such as PowerPoint, a laptop, charts or graphs, it's important that they are clear and informative.

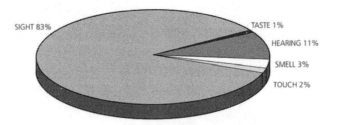

Impact on the brain of information from the senses during a visual presentation

One US study found that the retention of verbal presentations is only 10%. This means that a verbal presentation requires frequent repetition of key points to be effective. By comparison, the retention rate of combined verbal and visual presentations is 50%. This means you will achieve a 400% increase in efficiency through the use of visual aids in your business presentations.

Tip: If you are relying on 21st-century gadgets and technology, such as a piece of software, microphone, PowerPoint or a laptop, always check it before your presentation. Any failure will reflect badly on you, whether or not it is your fault. Always have a back-up option in case things don't go according to plan.

BODY LANGUAGE AT WORK FOR HER

Women hold more direct eye contact than men during business presentations when they (women) are not talking. When women are talking, however, they avert their eyes more than men do. When giving a presentation, women should beware of looking down towards the ground or lowering the head too frequently, as both actions send a submissive signal. Women should practise holding their head up and maintaining eye contact when speaking if they want to look authoritative and confident.

Princess Diana mastered the art of demurely lowering her head and looking up submissively. It worked wonders to evoke sympathy in the public, but would have been a disaster in a business presentation.

BODY LANGUAGE AT WORK FOR HIM

Pay attention to how you stand when giving a presentation or waiting for your turn to speak. Some men who are lacking in confidence will stand in the **Broken-Zipper** position, particularly if they are presenting as a group and another colleague is talking. This position makes them feel secure because they can protect their Crown Jewels and can symbolically avoid the consequences of a nasty frontal blow. It conveys an insecurity and vulnerability. You should also avoid crossing one leg in front of the other in standing, known as the **Scissors**. Both positions convey a defensive, insecure or closed attitude, whereas standing with your legs slightly apart and your arms relaxed shows openness or dominance, and conveys a much more positive attitude to your audience.

> **Open legs show male confidence;
> closed legs show male reticence.**

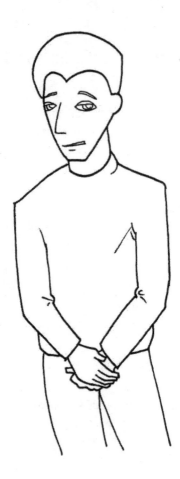

The Broken-Zipper position

Look your audience in the eye

> Making eye contact with your audience will increase their trust in your credibility.

As professional conference speakers, we developed a technique for keeping an audience's attention and letting them feel involved. In groups of up to 50 people it's possible to meet the gaze of each individual. In larger groups you usually stand further back, so a different approach is needed. By pegging a real or imaginary point or person at each corner of the group and one in the centre, when you stand at a distance of 10 metres from the front row, approximately 20 people in a group of up to 50 will feel you are looking at them individually as you speak and you will create an intimate bond with them. A valuable tip when you need to get your colleagues or clients on side.

Tip: When giving a presentation via a video camera, take some time beforehand to get the positioning of the camera perfect so that when your associates watch you, you will be looking directly at them. Eye contact is such an important part of communication that it really pays to get the camera angle right. Many cameras are placed on top of a computer monitor, which means that – to your business associates – you will be looking down if you are looking ahead at the monitor. This can present a negative impression. Ideally, the camera should be placed directly in front of the eyes.

Why women need to straight-talk in business

Because women evolved as nurturers, their speech and language are designed to avoid confrontation and to build relationships. They are also capable of multi-tracking, so can weave many threads into a conversation. This means that women tend to use more words than men to make a point, will hint at what they want, rather than saying it directly and can talk about several different things at once. This worked well for women in the past, because it stopped them sounding aggressive. However, when a woman uses indirect speech in business, it can be problematic, because men have difficulty following an indirect conversation. A woman can have her ideas and requests rejected purely because her male colleagues didn't have a clue what she wanted. Marie was the classic victim.

After six months of negotiations, Marie finally won the chance to present her company's new advertising programme to a major client. The audience would be eight men and four women, the account up for grabs was worth $200,000 and she had 30 minutes to sell her idea. Marie arrived perfectly dressed in a tailored, knee-length business suit, her hair was up, she wore light, natural make-up and she had practised her PowerPoint presentation so well that she could deliver it in her sleep.

As she started into her presentation, however, she noticed how blankly the men were looking at her. She felt they were judging her critically and, assuming they were losing interest, she began to multi-track her presentation to try to spur their interest by going back to previous images in PowerPoint, talking indirectly and trying to show how one related to the other. Most of the women were giving her encouragement by smiling at her and generally looking interested. Marie was excited by the women's feedback and started pitching her idea to them, unintentionally ignoring the men. Her presentation became a juggling act. She left convinced she'd done a great job and eagerly waited for the response.

Here's the conversation that later took place between the male executives:

Marketing director: 'Do you guys know what the hell she was talking about?'
Chief executive: 'No . . . she lost me. Tell her to send the proposal in writing.'

Marie had multi-tracked her presentation and used indirect talk with a group of men who didn't have a clue what she was talking about. The women executives were happy with the presentation, but no man wanted to admit he didn't follow it.

When a man can't follow a woman's business talk, he often pretends to understand.

Women need to be direct with men in business and give them one thing at a time to consider. Give him timetables, agendas, bottom-line answers and deadlines. Marie is still waiting for an answer . . .

Our top five pointers for perfect presentations

1. **Never tell the audience you feel anxious or over-awed:** they'll start looking for nervous body language and will be sure to find it. They'll never suspect you're nervous unless you tell them.

2. **Use confidence gestures as you speak,** even if you're feeling terrified. Use Steeple gestures, open and closed palm positions and keep your arms unfolded.

3. **Avoid negative gestures,** such as pointing at the audience, arm-crossing, feet-crossing, face-touching and lectern-gripping.

4. **Be expressive but don't overdo it.** Keep your fingers closed when you gesture, and your hands below chin level.

5. **Look animated.** Make sure your facial expressions mirror what you're saying. People are more likely to believe you and engage with you if your face tells the same story as your words. Take care not to go overboard.

The Steeple: a favourite of confident managerial types

Positive body language when giving presentations at work will enhance your credibility and make your audience more receptive to what you are saying.

Body Language at Work

Rule No. 7

Mirroring someone's body-language gestures is an excellent strategy to use if you are part of a presentation team at work. Decide, in advance, that when the team spokesperson makes a gesture or takes a posture while speaking, the entire group will mirror. This not only gives your team the powerful appearance of being cohesive, it can frighten the hell out of competitors, who suspect something is up even though they can't quite figure out what it is.

Body Language at Work

If you are delivering a work presentation or speech, make a point of looking at whether your audience have their heads up or down. When you see an audience tilting their heads and leaning forward using hand-to-chin evaluation gestures, you're getting the point across. If, however, you see that most people have their heads bowed, you will need to take action to involve your audience and get participation. Many professional speakers begin by involving their audience in some way. This is intended to get the audience's heads up and to ensure involvement.

How to spot when you are losing an audience's interest

Pay attention to your audience's body language in work presentations. This will tell you whether your delivery is going well, or if you need to take a different tack to gain audience involvement. Don't just blunder on. Negative signs to look out for include:

- **Darting Eyes.** This can look as if the person is checking out the activity in the room, but in fact the brain is searching for escape routes.

- **The Tight-Lipped Smile.** If you are in a smaller group, the person might use a Tight-Lipped Smile to feign interest because most of us are aware that looking away shows a lack of interest in the other person and is rude.

- **Crossed arms.** This has the same defensive, negative meaning everywhere. It's a person's attempt to put a barrier between themselves and something they don't like. Experienced speakers know that this gesture means a good 'ice-breaker' is needed to move their audience into a more receptive position.

Tip: If you are conducting a presentation by video link-up, you'll need to be even more aware of your audience's reactions as you won't be able to see the nuances of their body language. Look out for arm-crossing and leaning away from the screen. Creating a personal rapport is key, and always make sure that they can see and hear you properly before you begin. There's nothing worse than having to stop and start a presentation due to a technical glitch.

Mastering Meetings and Perfecting Phone- and Video-Conferencing

Mark thought the business meeting was going extremely well.
Unfortunately, he hadn't noticed that for the past 20 minutes
his colleague's legs had been crossed away from him and pointing towards the nearest exit.

Be upstanding to be outstanding

Conduct all short-term decision-making meetings standing up. Studies show that standing conversations are significantly shorter than sitting ones and the person who conducts a standing meeting is perceived as having higher status than those who sit. Some cutting-edge businesses have even introduced a company policy of conducting short meetings standing up as it makes employees more dynamic.

Standing whenever others enter your work space is also an excellent timesaver, so consider having no visitors' chairs in your own work area. Standing decisions are quick and to the point, and others don't waste your time with social chatter or questions such as 'How's the family?' It's also a good idea to stand when speaking on the phone, as your words will sound more authoritative and you'll think more quickly.

Use the Power-Lift

To focus a person's attention in a one-to-one meeting, use a pen to point to a visual aid, whether a graph or a laptop, and, at the same time, verbalise what they see. Next, lift the pen and hold it between the other person's eyes and your eyes. This has the magnetic effect of lifting their head so that now they are looking at you and they see and hear what you are saying, achieving maximum absorption of your message. Keep the palm of your other hand open when you are speaking.

The Power-Lift – using a pen to control where a person looks in a meeting

Body Language at Work   Rule No. 9

Sitting with your elbows on the armrest of a chair is a position of power and conveys a strong, upright image. Humble, defeated individuals let the arms drop inside the arms of the chair, so avoid this at all times unless your goal is to appear defeated and fearful.

Body Language at Work   **Rule No. 10**

Use the Head-Tilt when listening to others, as it makes you appear non-threatening and intuitive. The listener will begin to feel trusting towards you. In business negotiations with men, however, businesswomen should keep their head up at all times to avoid looking submissive.

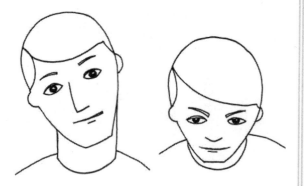

A useful gesture for businessmen who want to appear
non-threatening, but a no-no for businesswomen

Succeeding at phone-conferencing

Thanks to globalisation and the increase in working from home, most offices now use phone-conferencing and software such as Skype to conduct meetings. Because voice is often your only medium of communication, as you can't see your colleagues and clients, it can be much more difficult to read their cues. Take care to wait for pauses before speaking, which can be tricky if there is a delay. There's nothing worse than several people talking over one another. Equally, make it clear when you have finished talking. Try finishing a point with 'What are your thoughts on that?' This gives the other person or people a clear marker that it is their turn to speak and shows that you are leading the discussion.

Women should practise using a deeper voice for phone-conferencing to establish greater credibility.

How phone calls build rapport

When conducting business over the phone, pay attention to the intonation, voice inflection and speed of speaking of the other person. Never speak at a faster rate than them. Studies reveal that others describe feeling 'pressured' when someone speaks more quickly than they do. A person's speed of speech shows the rate at which their brain can consciously analyse information. Speak at the same rate or slightly slower than the other person and mirror their inflection and intonation. If you can synchronise your speech patterns with that of the other person, it helps to further establish mutual attitudes and build rapport. This is known as 'pacing' and it can almost seem as if the two people are singing in tune. As a business relationship grows over time, the mirroring of the main body-language positions becomes less as each person begins to anticipate the other's attitudes, and vocal pacing with the other person becomes a main medium for maintaining rapport.

Make it your business to look under the desk . . .

The further away from the brain a body part is positioned, the less awareness we have of what it is doing. This means that the legs and feet are an important source of information about someone's attitude. In a meeting or negotiation, a person can look composed and in control while under the desk their foot is repetitively tapping or making short jabs in the air, revealing their frustration at not being able to escape.

We conducted a series of tests with managers, who were instructed to lie convincingly in a set of staged interviews. We found that the managers, regardless of gender, dramatically increased the unconscious number of foot movements they made when they were lying. Most managers used fake facial expressions and tried to control their hands while lying, but almost all were unaware of what their feet and legs were doing. So if your boss is telling you that no one at the company, not even him, will be getting a pay rise this year, be sure to look under the desk to see if he's telling the truth.

Psychologist Paul Ekman discovered that not only do people increase their lower body movements when they lie, but observers have greater success exposing a person's lies when they can see the liar's entire body. This explains why many business executives feel comfortable only when sitting behind a desk with a solid front, where their lower body is hidden.

. . . and to look at their legs

The legs evolved in humans to serve two purposes: to move forward to get food and to run away from danger. Because the human brain is hardwired for these two objectives – to go towards what we want and move away from what we don't want – the way a person uses their legs and feet reveals where they want to go. In other words, they show a person's commitment to leaving or staying in a conversation. Open or uncrossed leg positions show an open or dominant attitude, while crossed positions reveal closed attitudes or uncertainty. If you're in a business meeting and your colleague or client has their feet pointed towards the nearest exit, it's a signal that you should do something to get the person involved and interested, or else terminate the meeting on your terms, allowing you to maintain control.

> If you're in a meeting and aren't sure whether you're being lied to or not, look under the desk.

Why refreshments can seal a deal

Offering a refreshment during a business negotiation or meeting is an excellent strategy for gauging how the other person is receiving your views or offer. Where a person places their cup immediately after they take a drink is a strong indicator of whether or not they are convinced or open to what you are saying. Someone who is feeling hesitant, unsure or negative about what they are hearing will place their cup in front of their body to form a barrier. When they accept what they are hearing, they will place the cup to the side of their body, showing an open or receptive attitude.

The arm barrier says, 'No.'

She's now open to your ideas.

How to get a decision over dinner

Today, business decisions are just as likely to be made outside the work place as they are inside, so let's consider the dynamics of encouraging a favourable response to a business proposition in a restaurant. Getting a positive decision is easier when the other person is relaxed and their barriers have been lowered. A few simple rules need to be followed:

- **Sit the other person with their back to a solid wall or screen.** It reduces stress and tension.
- **Opt for a venue with a relaxing atmosphere,** with dimmed lighting and muffled background music. Top restaurants often have an open fireplace or fire facsimile, as they know that a relaxed customer spends more money.

'Why am I holding all these pens, pencils and brochures?' asked the customer, who had begun to look like a decorated Christmas tree. 'I'll come to that later,' said the salesman.

- **Choose a round table and limit distractions.** Have your companion's view of other people obscured by a screen or large green plant if you want a captive audience, and avoid noisy tables near the kitchen or bar.

- **Complete most of the discussion before the food arrives.** Conversation can come to a standstill once you start eating, and alcohol dulls the brain. After you've eaten, the stomach takes blood away from the brain to help digestion, making it harder for people to think clearly. Present your proposals while everyone is alert.

> No one ever makes a business decision with their mouth full.

Body Language at Work   **Rule No. 11**

Watch their coat buttons. Analysis of videotaped confrontations, for example, between unions and corporations, show a higher frequency of agreement is reached when people have their coats unbuttoned. People who cross their arms on their chest often do it with their jacket buttoned and are more negative. When a person suddenly unbuttons their jacket in a meeting, you can reasonably assume that they have also just opened their mind.

Body Language at Work   Rule No. 12

If you're in a meeting or sales negotiation and see that your listener's body language has become defensive – for instance, arm-crossing, sitting back or leaning away – a simple but effective way of breaking the negative position is to give the listener something to hold or do. Handing them a pen, book, brochure, sample or written test forces them to unfold their arms and lean forward. This moves them into a more open position and, therefore, a more open attitude. Asking someone to lean forward to look at a laptop can also be an effective means of opening a defensive posture. You could even lean forward with your palms up and say, 'I can see you have a question . . . What would you like to know?' or, 'What's your opinion?' You then sit or lean back to indicate that it's their turn to speak. By using your palms, you non-verbally tell them that you would like them to be open and honest because that's what you're being.

Our top five musts for mastering meetings

1. **Keep your fingers together.** People who keep their fingers closed when they gesture with their hands and keep their hands below chin level command the most attention and are deemed more powerful.

2. **Subtly mirror the other person,** including their seating position, posture, body angle, gestures, expressions and tone of voice. This is one of the most powerful ways to build rapport quickly. They'll start to feel that there's something about you they like and they'll be in a more receptive and relaxed frame of mind.

3. **Don't sit too close to your colleague or client.** As a rule, you can move closer to familiar people but further back from new ones. Men generally move closer to women they work with, while women move further back from men.

> Using visual aids, like PowerPoint and laptops, cuts the average business meeting time from 25.7 minutes to 18.6 minutes – a 28% time saving.

4. **Nod your head:** it's a powerful persuasion tool. Slow nodding communicates that the listener is interested in what the speaker is saying, so give slow, deliberate clusters of three nods when the other person is making a point. Fast nodding tells the speaker you've heard enough or that you want them to finish or give you a turn to speak.

5. **Practise and visualise positive body language.** Before you go to an important meeting, sit quietly for five minutes and mentally rehearse seeing yourself doing these things and doing them well. When your mind sees them clearly, your body will be able to carry them out and others will react accordingly.

Finally, know when to end a meeting

Gestures that signal a desire to conclude a meeting include leaning forward with both hands on both knees or leaning forward with both hands gripping the chair as if the person were at the start of a race. If either of these occur during a meeting, it would be wise for you to take the lead and resell, change direction or terminate the conversation.

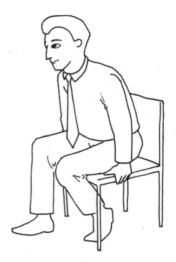

On your marks, get set: in the starting blocks –
change tack or this meeting is over

The Best-Kept Secrets of Successful Businesspeople

Some people described Roger as the backbone of the organisation. Others didn't go that high.

Put yourself head and shoulders above the competition . . .

> Tall people not only get the best jobs in American firms, they also receive higher starting salaries: in one study, those over 6 feet 2 inches got 12% more than those under 6 feet.

Despite what it may be politically correct to believe, studies convincingly show that taller people are more successful than short people. We constantly observe how top-level managers are significantly taller than everyone else. Height is also linked to financial success: our research found that every inch of height above the company norm added almost £400 to that person's salary, regardless of the person's sex.

Height differences have a significant impact on business dealings, but height and power are often just perceptions. If you are a shorter person, there are several strategies you can employ to neutralise the power of taller people who set out to intimidate you. This is important if you are a woman because women are, on average, 2 inches shorter than men.

As a woman, the shorter you are, the more likely it is that you will be interrupted by men. Stand up when giving presentations and you'll instantly have more authority.

. . . with our top five tips for looking taller and more powerful . . .

1. **Control the environment** by having chairs of varying heights and asking tall people to sit on the lower chairs because sitting neutralises height. Sitting the Incredible Hulk on a low sofa diminishes his perceived power.

2. **Sit at opposite ends of a table** to even things up, or lean in someone's office doorway to talk while they are seated.

3. **Tackle overbearing colleagues who stand over you** by getting up, walking over to a window and gazing outside as you discuss an issue. You will look as if you are giving deep consideration to the discussion and the bigger person can't have a height advantage when you aren't looking at them.

Napoleon was just 5 feet 4 inches tall, but those who see paintings of him perceive him as over 6 inches taller.

4. **Act assertively.** Standing erect, sitting up straight and 'walking tall' are ways of giving yourself a confident appearance and, because of the law of cause and effect, you will feel more confident when you do these things.

5. **Increase your perceived height** and be more likely to be remembered as taller by wearing dark-coloured clothing, pinstriped suits or trouser suits, softer, more muted make-up (for women) and full-size chronograph watches. The smaller the watch size, the less clout a person is perceived to have.

... but don't get too big for your boots

Being tall, however, is not always a bonus in business. While tall people often command more respect than short people, height can also be detrimental to some aspects of one-to-one communication, for instance where you need to 'talk on the same level' or have an 'eye-to-eye' discussion with a colleague and do not want be perceived as 'too big for your boots'.

In Britain, Philip Heinicy, a 6-feet-8 inch chemicals salesperson, formed the Tall Person's Club to meet the needs of the taller members of society. He found that his height was threatening to his customers; they felt imposed upon and could not concentrate on what he had to say. He discovered that when he gave a sales presentation in a seated position, not only did the atmosphere become more conducive to good communication, the removal of his physical threat also increased his bottom-line sales by a whopping 62%.

 Tip: If you're particularly tall or if you want to create a relaxed atmosphere in which to build rapport, then conduct meetings and presentations sitting down.

Why Clark Kent is more powerful than Superman

In one study, people pictured wearing glasses were judged by respondents as being 14 IQ points more intelligent compared to when they were not wearing them. In fact, when you add glasses to a face in a business context, respondents describe that person as 'studious', 'intelligent', 'conservative', 'educated' and 'sincere'. It's little surprise that Superman wears glasses when he transforms himself into his alter-ego, the journalist Clark Kent. In business, glasses are a statement of power. Frameless, small or spindly frames convey a powerless image and say that you are more interested in fashion than business. Having a pair of non-prescription glasses could be an excellent strategy for business meetings. Avoid glasses with oversized lenses, Elton John-style coloured frames or designer glasses with distracting initials on the frame.

> People in positions of power should wear stronger frames to make serious points, such as reading a financial budget, and frameless styles when conveying a 'nice guy' image or being 'one of the boys'.

Tip: If you wear glasses, remove them when speaking and put them back on to listen. This not only relaxes the other person, but allows you to have control of the conversation. The listener quickly becomes conditioned that when you take your glasses off, you're taking the floor, and when you put them back on, it's their turn to talk.

Tip: 'Dress-down Friday' is a modern business phenomenon that encourages employees to wear casual clothes one day a week. Successful people, however, know how important it is to maintain a professional image at work and simply ignore HR initiatives that encourage them to dress like they're going to the beach when they're going to sit in a boardroom all day.

Harness the power of NLP

A person's eye movements (whether upwards, to the side, down to the right or down to the left) can reveal what their mind is focusing on by telling you whether they are remembering something they have seen, heard, smelled, tasted or touched. This technique is known as neurolinguistic programming, or NLP, and could give your career a real boost.

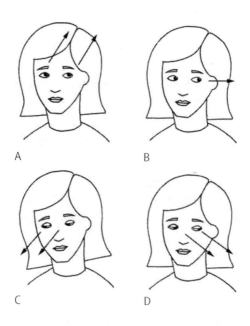

A. Recalling a picture   B. Recalling a sound
C. Recalling a feeling   D. Talking to oneself

Learning how to read these split-second movements will tell you how to adapt your language to communicate effectively in business. For instance, someone who looks up, indicating that they are recalling a picture, prefers the visual information channel and will use phrases such as 'I see what you mean' and 'Can you show me that?' You will get their attention by showing them photos, charts and graphs, and asking if they 'get the picture'. People who prefer the feelings channel and say things like 'Let's kick that idea around' and 'Our department needs a shot in the arm' will love to test-drive things and be involved in a demonstration so that they can 'grasp the idea'. By understanding your colleagues and customers, you'll be able to adapt your approach to suit the individual.

NLP is a remarkable discovery and a powerful communications tool that should be addressed as a separate subject. We suggest you follow up by researching NLP.

BODY LANGUAGE AT WORK FOR HER

Contact lenses can reflect lights, give you a softer, more sensual appearance and make your pupils appear dilated. Because pupil size increases when people view something that stimulates or arouses them, wearing contacts can be disastrous in business, especially for women. A woman can find herself trying her best to persuade a businessman to buy her ideas while he is mesmerised by the sensual effect of her contact lenses and doesn't hear a word she says. Women would do better to wear glasses in business situations than contact lenses.

BODY LANGUAGE AT WORK FOR HIM

The size of a briefcase is linked to perceptions of the status of its owner. Those who carry large, bulging briefcases are thought to do all the work and probably take work home because they are poor time-managers. Slim briefcases say that the owner is only concerned with the bottom line and therefore has more status. Successful businessmen therefore carry slender briefcases or no briefcase at all.

Top professionals know how to see eye to eye

> It is only when you see 'eye to eye' with another person that a real basis for communication can be established.

Succeeding in today's cut-throat business world has a lot to do with building relationships. While some people can make us feel comfortable when they talk with us, others make us feel ill at ease, and some seem untrustworthy. Initially, this has to do with the length of time that they look at us or how long they hold our gaze as they speak. In most cultures, to build a good rapport with another person, your gaze should meet theirs about 60–70% of the time. This will also cause them to begin to like you. It is not surprising, therefore, that the nervous, timid salesman who meets our gaze less than a third of the time is rarely trusted. This is also why, in negotiations, dark-tinted glasses should be avoided, as they make others feel you are either staring at them or trying to avoid them. People who wear dark sunglasses during meetings, even outdoor ones, are seen as suspicious, secretive and insecure.

Tip: when negotiating in foreign countries, always observe the amount of eye contact that is used in business and mirror it. Japanese and South Americans lock eyes less than Europeans and Westerners, who can be perceived as aggressive.

Tip: Never underestimate the value of owning high-status gadgets. Carrying a BlackBerry or the latest 4G phone with you shows that you are important enough to need to be available at all times . . . Just remember to turn it off before meetings, and avoid gimmicky ringtones and personal calls.

Why the world's leading businesswomen are made up

It may not be PC to say so, but research shows that wearing make-up adds to perceived credibility for women in business. To demonstrate this, we hired four similar-looking female assistants to help sell our training products at a seminar. One wore glasses and make-up, the second wore glasses and no make-up, the third had make-up and no glasses and the fourth had neither. Customers were asked to choose adjectives from a list that best described each woman. The woman wearing both make-up and glasses was described as 'confident', 'intelligent', 'sophisticated' and 'outgoing'. The assistant who wore make-up and no glasses received good ratings on appearance but lower on personal skills such as listening and building rapport. The assistants who wore no make-up were rated worst on personal skills and personal presentation, and wearing glasses without make-up made little difference to the customers' attitudes and recall.

The bottom line here is clear: make-up gives the impression of more intelligence and confidence, and the combination of glasses and make-up in business has the most positive and memorable impact on observers. Businesswomen should take care, however, not to wear heavy make-up or they risk looking too interested in men's attention and in themselves. Natural, neutral make-up shows they mean business.

Office jargon and corporate-speak

While it pays to familiarise yourself with the language and terminology of your particular industry, you should be wary of using the kind of corporate-speak that alienates people, sounds clichéd or nonsensical and obscures meaning. Expressions like 'pushing the envelope', 'going forward', 'thinking outside the box', 'blue-sky thinking' and 'right-sizing' (meaning redundancies) are liable to make you sound like you've swallowed a management guide, and a bad one at that. They are essentially examples of indirect speech and have negative associations for most people. On the other hand, simple but direct language can be well worth incorporating into your daily vocabulary. Power words like 'save', 'new', 'results', 'easy' and 'safety' are very persuasive and are proven to have a positive impact.

Expert emails

Email has now replaced the telephone as the main source of business communication so it's important to get the tone right. Emails, like texts, encourage the sender to use informal, jokey language and punctuation, effectively lulling you into a false sense of security. Women in particular need to pay attention to the tone of their emails. Being prone to indirect talk – using too many words and complex thought patterns – women need to keep emails short and succinct. And both sexes should steer well clear of swear words, slang, text-speak and affectionate sign-offs if they want to be taken seriously. If the MD wouldn't use it, neither should you. Avoid gossiping or inappropriate messages, even between friends at work. We all know how easy it is to send a message accidentally to the wrong person, if not the whole company.

Tip: Being au fait with the latest technology and software – PowerPoint, Skype, Facebook and the office database and systems – will enhance your credibility at work and give you a reputation for being at the cutting edge. Take the time to familiarise yourself with technical language and software and you'll soon be seen as a 21st-century person who is forward-thinking.

Master the business of smiling

Social psychologist Dr Nancy Henley found that, in social encounters, women smile 87% of the time versus 67% for men. An experiment using 15 photographs of women showing happy, sad and neutral faces were rated by 257 respondents. Pictures of unsmiling women were decoded as a sign of unhappiness, while pictures of unsmiling men were seen as a sign of dominance. The lessons here are for women to smile less when dealing with dominant men in business or to mirror the amount of smiling that men do. And if men want to be more persuasive with women in business, they need to smile more.

> Businesswomen who smile too much can be regarded as submissive and as pacifiers because a woman's smile is 'her badge of appeasement' and is often used to placate a more powerful male.

Globalisation:
the Perils and the Pitfalls

Brian couldn't understand why his Arab business
acquaintances had suddenly walked out of the meeting . . .
until someone explained that instead of giving them the
go-ahead for the multi-million-dollar deal, he had just
gestured an obscenity.

A tricky business

Learning the intricacies of foreign body-language gestures can be a tricky, and potentially humiliating, business.

The 21st-century work place is truly global. Nowadays, we think nothing of a business trip to China, video-conferencing with an outsourced department in India and attending conferences in the US. Surprisingly, though, very few of today's professionals take the time to learn international body-language customs. When it comes to doing international business, smart attire, excellent references and a good proposal can all become instantly unstuck by the smallest, most innocent gesture sinking the whole deal. Our research in 42 countries shows Americans to be the least culturally sensitive people, with the British coming in a close second. Considering that 86% of Americans don't have a pass-port, including George W. Bush when he became president, it's perhaps not surprising. Though the Brits travel extensively and do business with many different cultures, they still prefer everyone else to use British body signals, speak English and serve fish and chips.

Foreign business associates are extremely impressed if you have taken the time to learn and use their body-language customs. People do business with people who make them feel comfortable and it comes down to sincerity and good manners. If you are entering a foreign country on business, concentrate on reducing the broadness of your body language until you have the opportunity to observe your hosts.

> In today's global work place, you should make it a priority to learn and respect the body language of your business associates if you want to impress them and avoid embarrassing moments.

The deal-maker and the deal-breaker

The 'OK' or 'perfect' gesture (see page 135) was popularised in the US during the early 19th century and its meaning is common to all English-speaking countries, but it has other origins and connotations in certain places. For example, in France and Belgium it also means 'zero' or 'nothing'. In a Paris restaurant one evening, the waiter showed us to our table and asked, 'Is the table OK?' We flashed him the OK signal and he responded, 'Well, if you don't like it here, we'll find you another table . . .' He had interpreted the OK signal as meaning 'zero' or 'worthless' – in other words, he thought we had communicated that we didn't like the table.

In Japan, it can mean 'money', so if you're doing business in Japan and you make this sign for 'OK', a Japanese may think you're asking them for a bribe! In some Mediterranean countries, it's an orifice signal, often used to infer that a man is homosexual. Show a Greek businessman the OK signal and he may think you're inferring you or he is gay, while a Turk might think you're calling him an 'arsehole'. It's rare in Arab countries, where it is used as either a threat signal or as an obscenity. Being unaware of local body-language customs can have disastrous consequences. An American businessman might think he is sealing a deal but in fact he has just told his Turkish business contacts, 'You're all a bunch of arseholes'!

Three gestures to avoid in business

This can mean 'Two' to an American business person, 'Victory' to a German and 'Up yours' to a Brit.

A Western businessperson would use this to signal 'Two', but to their Greek counterpart this means 'Go to hell!'

Your British or Australian boss might use this to indicate 'One', but to their European colleague it could mean 'Two', and their Japanese customer has just been on the receiving end of a nasty insult!

You say hello; I say goodbye

Handshaking differences can make for some embarrassing and disastrous business encounters. British, Australian, German and American colleagues will usually shake hands on meeting, and again on departure. Most Europeans will shake hands with each other several times a day, and some French have been noted to shake hands for up to 30 minutes a day. Indian, Asian and Arabic businesspeople may continue to hold your hand when the handshake has ended. Germans and French give one or two firm pumps followed by a short hold, whereas Brits give three to five pumps compared with an American's five to seven pumps. This is hilarious to observe at international conferences where a range of different handshake pumping takes place between surprised delegates! And don't even get us started on those who greet with a kiss! When shaking hands with other cultures, follow the lead of the other person and adapt accordingly if you want your business meeting to be a hit.

To the Americans, the German businesspeople, with their single pump, seem distant. To the Germans, however, the Americans pump hands as if they are blowing up an airbed.

One area where handshakes have not become established is Japan, where such bodily contact can be considered impolite. Japanese people bow on first meeting, the person with the highest status bowing the least and the one with the least status bowing the most. On first meeting, business cards are exchanged, each person assesses the other's status and appropriate bowing follows. Do not put a Japanese person's business card into your trouser pocket. This can be seen as offensive.

When doing business in Japan, make sure your shoes are spotlessly clean and in good condition. Every time a Japanese businessman bows, he inspects them.

You say yes; I say no

The Japanese way of listening to someone involves a repertoire of smiles, nods and polite noises, which have no direct equivalent in other languages. The idea is to encourage you to keep on talking, but this is often misinterpreted by Western businesspeople as agreement. The head-nod is an almost universal sign for 'yes', though the Japanese use it for politeness.

If you say something a Japanese businessman doesn't agree with, he'll still say, 'Yes' – or '*Hai*' in Japanese – to keep you talking. A Japanese 'Yes' usually means 'Yes, I heard you' and not necessarily 'Yes, I agree'. For example, if you say to a Japanese businessman, 'You don't agree, do you?' he will nod his head and say, 'Yes,' even though he may not agree. In the Japanese context, it means 'Yes, you are correct – I don't agree'.

Arguably the two simplest words are 'yes' and 'no', but even these can lead to some tortuous misunderstandings when different nationalities do business.

The Japanese are concerned with saving face and have developed a set of rules to prevent things going wrong, so try to avoid saying no or asking questions when the answer might be no. The closest a Japanese will get to saying the word 'no' is 'It is very difficult' or 'We will give this positive study' when they really mean 'Let's forget the whole thing and go home'.

In India, the head is rocked from side to side, called the Head-Wobble, to signal 'Yes'. This is confusing for Westerners and Europeans, who use this gesture to communicate 'Maybe yes – maybe no'.

In Arab countries, they use a single, upward head movement, which means 'No'.

Beware of doing business in Bulgaria, where a head-nod means 'No' and a head-shake means 'Yes'.

Why Japanese businesspeople lead the waltz

At our international conferences, city-born Americans usually stand 18–48 inches from each other and stand in the same place while talking. If you watch a Japanese and an American businessman talking, the two will slowly begin to move around the room, the American moving backwards away from the Japanese and the Japanese moving forwards. This is an attempt by both the American and the Japanese to adjust to a culturally comfortable distance from the other. The Japanese, with his smaller 10-inch Intimate Zone, continually steps forwards to adjust to his spatial need, but this invades the American's Intimate Zone, forcing him to step backwards to make his own spatial adjustment. Video recordings of this phenomenon replayed at high speed give the illusion that the two men are waltzing round the room with the Japanese leading. This is one of the reasons why, when negotiating business, Asians, Europeans or Americans often look at each other with suspicion.

In business, Westerners refer to the Asians as 'pushy' and 'familiar', and the Asians refer to the Europeans or Americans as 'cold', 'stand-offish' and 'cool'.

Why colds can be bad for business

Europeans and Westerners blow their noses into a handkerchief or tissue, while Asians and Japanese spit or snort. Each is appalled by what they see as the other's 'disgusting' behaviour. This dramatic cultural difference is the direct result of the spread of tuberculosis in past centuries. In Europe, someone who contracted tuberculosis had little hope of survival, so governments instructed people to blow their nose to avoid further spreading the disease. This is why Westerners react so strongly to spitting – a spitting person could spread tuberculosis.

Because tuberculosis wasn't such a problem in Eastern countries, Asians believe, correctly, that it is a healthier option to spit. As a result, the Japanese are appalled when someone produces a handkerchief, blows their nose into it and puts it back in their pocket, purse or up their sleeve! The Japanese are also unimpressed at the English custom of businessmen wearing a handkerchief in their jacket top pocket. This is the equivalent of proudly dangling a roll of toilet paper from the pocket, ready for action. On the other hand, spitting is a habit that is repulsive to Westerners. This is why business meetings between Westerners and Asians can fail when they've all got a cold.

When we talk, we maintain 40–60% eye contact with an average of 80% eye contact when listening. The notable exception to this rule is Japan and some Asian and South American cultures, where extended eye contact is seen as aggressive or disrespectful. The Japanese tend to look away or at your throat, which can be disconcerting for culturally inexperienced Western businesspeople. The safest rule when doing business with other nationalities, such as the Japanese, is to mirror the gaze time of the other person.

Don't feel upset by an Asian businessman who spits or snorts, and never blow your nose in front of a Japanese associate.

Office Politics, Power-Players, Office Romances and Other Ticking Bombs

John got the distinct feeling that his boss wasn't taking his application for a promotion entirely seriously.

Beat superior types at their own game . . .

Accountants, lawyers, managers and the real scourge of the 21st-century work place, business consultants, are notorious for using superiority body-language clusters around people they consider inferior. Mirroring can be a highly effective strategy for intimidating or disarming these 'superior' types. By mirroring, you can disconcert them and force a change of position. A word of warning, though: never do it to the boss. Your manager could feel affronted by your body language and your job could be in jeopardy.

A boss would perceive a subordinate's mirroring
behaviour as arrogance

... and intimidate the office power-player

Whether they're the HR manager, the health-and-safety rep, your boss or even your opposite number, every office contains power-players who intimidate or antagonise colleagues and try to take control of meetings and decisions. If you're confronted by an intimidating power-player, leaning against something can be used as a method of dominance if the object being leaned on belongs to them. An easy way to intimidate someone is to lean against, sit on or use their possessions without their permission. There are many intimidation techniques you can use at work. One is to lean against the doorway to another person's office or to sit in their chair. More subtle approaches include placing your foot hard against the leg of their desk or using someone's phone or computer to stake your claim on their property.

Some people are habitual doorway leaners and go through life unwittingly intimidating everyone from first introduction. These people are well advised to practise an upright stance with palms visible to create a favourable impression. Others form up to 90% of their opinion about us in the first four minutes and you never get a second chance to make a first impression.

The office doorway intimidator

Body Language at Work   **Rule No. 13**

The **Power Gaze** works a treat on the person who you want to intimidate or on the office bore who simply won't shut up. Imagine the person has a third eye in the centre of their forehead and look in a triangular area between the person's 'three' eyes. The impact this gaze has on the other person has to be experienced to be believed. Not only does it change the atmosphere to very serious, it can stop a bore dead in their tracks. By keeping your gaze directed at this area, you keep the screws firmly on them. Provided your gaze doesn't drop below the level of their eyes, the pressure will stay on them. It's a great one for a manager who is going to reprimand an errant subordinate.

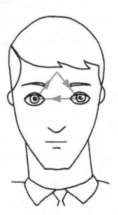

The Power Gaze

Body Language at Work

Rule No. 14

The **Power Stare** is only to be used if you need to give yourself more authority and are under attack from someone. When you look at the attacker, narrow your eyelids and focus closely on the person without blinking. This is what predatory animals do just before they strike their prey. When you pan your eyes from one person to another without blinking it has an unnerving effect on anyone who watches you do it. To do this, move your eyeballs first and then let your head follow, but your shoulders should remain still. The Power Stare was used by Arnold Schwarzenegger as the Terminator and can strike fear into the hearts of would-be intimidators. This gesture really is a last resort, so don't use it in business unless someone at work has truly overstepped the mark.

How to spot an office romance at 20 paces

Given how much time many of today's businesspeople spend in the office, it's hardly surprising that romance has become commonplace in the work place. Sometimes, it pays to be in the know, so use these pointers for working out whether love is in the air:

1. **Proximity.** The closer people feel emotionally to each other, the closer they will stand to each other.

2. **Ownership.** Look out for intimate gestures that subtly indicate a territorial claim to that person – a woman may brush lint from a man to show others that he is taken; a man may put his arm in the small of a woman's back to show he is protecting her.

3. **Flirtatious body language.** In women, this might be self-touching, such as stroking her neck when talking, pointing her knee towards the object of her affection when sitting, or preening herself by flicking her hair and licking her lips. In men, this could be tucking his thumbs in his belt, adjusting his clothing and extended gazing.

4. **Touch.** Watch for repeated or more affectionate touching. A hand touch indicates a higher level of intimacy than a touch on the arm.

Contending with indifferent bosses and clients

One body-language position you really don't want to see at work is the **Leg-Over-the-Arm-of-Chair**. It's mainly done by men because it uses the **Legs-Spread**. It not only signifies the man's ownership of the chair, it also signals that he has an informal, aggressive attitude. Let's say an employee has a personal problem and goes to ask his boss for advice. The boss listens, motionless, then leans back in his chair and puts one leg over the arm. The boss's attitude has now changed to lack of concern or indifference. In other words, he has little concern for the employee or his problem and he may even feel that his time is being wasted with the 'same old story'. As long as the boss's leg stays over the arm of the chair, his indifferent attitude will persist.

The Leg-Over-the-Arm-of-Chair can be particularly annoying when it occurs during negotiation, and it is vital to make that person change position because the longer they stay in it, the longer they will have an indifferent or aggressive attitude.

Tip: An easy way to get someone to change this position is to ask them to lean across and look at something. As it's almost always done by a male, if you have a wicked sense of humour, tell him there's a split in his trousers!

Dealing with business contacts who keep you waiting . . .

If someone keeps you waiting for more than 20 minutes, it is either disorganisation or a form of power-play. Keeping someone waiting is an effective way of reducing their status and enhancing the status of the person who is making them wait.

Tip: If you are going to a business meeting, take a laptop, iPhone, or office work, which shows that you are busy and are not prepared to be inconvenienced. When the person who has kept you waiting comes out to meet you, let them speak first, lift your head slowly from your work and greet them, then pack up smoothly and confidently. Another good strategy when made to wait is to take out some financial papers and a calculator and do calculations. When they call for you say, 'I'll be ready in a moment – I'll just finish these calculations.' Or you could make all your mobile-phone calls. The clear message you are sending is that you're a very busy person and are not being inconvenienced by their disorganisation. If you suspect the other person is playing a power game, arrange for an urgent call to be put through to you during your meeting. Take the call, loudly mention large amounts of money, drop in a well-known name or two, tell the caller you never settle for second best and that they are to report back to you as soon as possible. Hang up the phone, apologise for the interruption and continue as if nothing had happened. Hey, it works for James Bond . . . it'll work for you.

. . . or who interrupt a meeting

If another person takes a phone call during the meeting or a third person enters and begins what seems like a long conversation, take out your laptop, BlackBerry or office work and begin to read. This gives them privacy and demonstrates that you don't waste your time. If you feel the person is doing these things intentionally, take out your own mobile phone and make several important follow-up calls about important ventures.

Catching out work Web-surfers . . .

It's common knowledge that most people browse the Internet while at work, even doing their shopping and logging on to Facebook during office hours. A certain amount of illicit Web-surfing is to be expected, but some employees have been found to spend literally hours of their working day browsing the Net. So how can you tell if someone's really working as hard as they appear to be? Most people keep their computer screens angled away from you to hide what they're doing when they're meant to be working, making it difficult to tell who is working and who isn't. If you want to spot whether you've just interrupted someone who has been surreptitiously surfing the Net – perhaps you suspect an employee of shirking – look out for giveaways like collar-pulling, neck-scratching and eye-rubbing. These are all deceit gestures that indicate the person has something to hide or suspect they have been caught out.

Tip: If you're a work Internet-surfer, hitting the Windows key followed by the letter 'M' will instantly minimise any open screens, preventing colleagues from seeing what you were doing. Alternatively, you could simply just do the job you are being paid to do.

. . . and how to tell if someone is *really* working from home

New technology has enabled more employees to work from home, but it has also enabled the less reputable to take advantage – telling bosses and employees they are working from home when really they are planning to log into their email a few times between trips to the golf course and lunch out with friends. Spotting whether someone truly intends to *work* from home is simple if you know what to look out for. If someone covers their mouth while telling you of their plans to work from home, you can fairly suspect that work is the last thing on their mind. The **Mouth-Cover** reveals that the speaker is trying to suppress the deceitful words that are being said. Sometimes several fingers can cover the mouth, or sometimes one finger rests just below the mouth.

'I've got lots to get through tomorrow so I'd be better off
working from home'

Why a great boss has a great office

If you find your relationships with employees are tense and strained, or that staff are talking about you behind your back, consider the impact your office layout may be having. To make your office conducive to good employer–staff relations, try the following:

1. If your office has a glass partition, place your desk in front of it. Your office will appear bigger and you will be visible to those who enter. In this way, visitors will be greeted by you personally, not your desk or computer monitor.

2. Coat the glass partition with a mirror finish, allowing you to see out, but not permitting others to see in. This raises your status by securing your territory and creating a more intimate atmosphere inside the office.

3. Place the visitor's chair so that the visitor's back is facing a wall or corner, not an open door, making communication more open and providing protection for staff who feel insecure.

4. Have a low round table with three identical swivel chairs for informal meetings, so everyone feels equal.

Executive offices are designed by office designers, not by those who understand interaction between people. Study your own work-place layout and make the positive changes needed. Pretty soon staff will describe you as 'easygoing', a relaxed person to work with and a great boss. A good office layout could be just what your career needs.

Dealing with stress in the work place

Today's office environment can be very stressful, with deadlines, targets, office politics and heavy workloads all contributing to our stress levels. If you find yourself in a high-stress situation, such as being confronted by a difficult colleague or preparing to lead a meeting, try the Superiority-Confidence gesture. The Duke of Edinburgh and several other male members of the Royal Family are noted for their habit of walking with head up, chin out and one hand holding the other hand behind the back. This gesture is also used by MDs checking up on their subordinates, senior military personnel and anyone in a position of authority.

The emotions attached to this gesture are superiority, confidence and power. The person exposes their vulnerable stomach, heart, crotch and throat in a subconscious act of fearlessness. You'll begin to *feel* confident and even authoritative, as a result of cause and effect, thus lowering your stress levels.

If all else fails, appease your boss with this Pease tip

Under attack, we make ourselves appear smaller by hunching our shoulders, pulling our arms in close to the body, pressing our knees together and locking our ankles under a chair, dropping our chin to the chest to protect the throat and averting our gaze by looking away. These gestures activate an 'off switch' in the brain of the aggressor and the attack can be avoided. This is an ideal position to take if you are being reprimanded by a superior when you actually deserve the reprimand.

> The number-one work-place rule?
> Remember, your boss's jokes are *always* funny.

Conclusion

Communication through body language has been going on for millions of years but has only been scientifically studied to any extent in the last 30 years. Now, in the 21st century, body language is finally being 'discovered' by businesspeople throughout the world and is becoming part of formal business training everywhere. Unless you've had formal training, though, few people really think about how they come across to colleagues, customers and associates, or take the time to learn the basics of body language.

Globalisation, computers, mobiles and the latest technology have completely changed the landscape of today's work place, creating new challenges for today's businessperson. We hope this book has armed you with the knowledge you need to make a success of any business encounter.

Finally, we'd like to give you a quick run-down of the key body-language points that could be the difference between languishing on the bottom rung of the career ladder and climbing to the very top:

- **Handshakes:** the first few minutes of a business encounter can make or break a relationship. Take the time to practise handshake styles with your friends and you can quickly learn how to deliver a positive handshake every time. Keeping the palms held vertical and matching the other person's grip is usually perceived as a 10/10 handshake.

- **Eye contact:** learn where to direct your gaze and when to maintain eye contact or look away. This will enhance your credibility in business.

- **Mirror:** subtly mirror the body language of colleagues and associates.

- **Gestures:** avoid closed or defensive body language, such as arm- or feet-crossing.

- **Practise and visualise positive body language** – use nods when talking, the Head-Tilt when listening if you're male, keep your chin up and stand up straight.

- **A man in business** needs to beware of aggressive or over-dominant body language, such as the Catapult or Legs-Spread, but equally he mustn't go too far to the other extreme and risk being thought of as ineffectual.

- **A woman in business** doesn't need to act in a masculine way; she simply needs to avoid signals of femaleness such as soft handshakes, short skirts and high heels if she wants equal credibility.

- **Avoid business expressions** like 'blue-sky thinking', 'incentivise' and 'thinking outside the box'. You'll either look outdated or faddish and people will distrust you. And never say 'modern' as this just tells people you're not.

- **Take advantage of the latest technology.** A top-of-the-range laptop, iPhone or BlackBerry will give you a status boost, and showing you are knowledgeable about IT, video-conferencing and PowerPoint will make you look professional and savvy.

Research has now shown convincingly that if you change your body language, you can change many things about your approach to life. You can feel more confident at work, become more likeable, be more persuasive or convincing and appear more professional. When you change your body language, you interact differently with people around you and they, in turn, will respond differently to you. It *is* possible to change your body language. Pay attention to how you present yourself at work and interact with others, and watch your credibility and status soar!

A successful businessperson is one who understands that their body language is every bit as important as what they say.

Why not use Allan Pease as guest speaker for your next conference or seminar?

PEASE INTERNATIONAL PTY LTD

PO Box 1260, Buderim 4556, Queensland, AUSTRALIA
Tel: +61 7 5445 5600
Email: info@peaseinternational.com
Website: www.peaseinternational.com

Allan and Barbara Pease are the most successful relationship authors in the business. They have written a total of 15 bestsellers - including 9 number ones - and give seminars in up to 30 countries each year. Their books are available in over 100 countries, are translated into 51 languages and have sold over 25 million copies. They appear regularly in the media worldwide and their work has been the subject of 9 television series, a stage play and a number one box office movie which attracted a combined audience of over 100 million.

Their company, Pease International Ltd, produces videos, training courses and seminars for business and governments worldwide. Their monthly relationship column was read by over 20 million people in 25 countries. They have 6 children and 5 grandkids and are based in Australia and the UK.

Also by Allan Pease:

DVD Programs
Body Language Series
Silent Signals Series
How To Be A People Magnet - It's Easy
 Peasey
The Best Of Body Language
How To Develop Powerful
 Communication Skills - Managing the
 Differences Between Men & Women

Audio Programs
The Definitive Book Of Body Language
Why Men Don't Listen & Women Can't
 Read Maps
Why Men Don't Have A Clue & Women
 Always Need More Shoes
How To Make Appointments By
 Telephone
Questions Are The Answers
It's Not What You Say

Books
The Definitive Book Of Body Language
Why Men Don't Listen & Women Can't
 Read Maps
Why Men Don't Have A Clue & Women
 Always Need More Shoes!
Why Men Want Sex & Women Need
 Love
Easy Peasey - People Skills For Life
Questions Are The Answers
Why He's So Last Minute & She's Got It
 All Wrapped Up
Why Men Can Only Do One Thing At A
 Time & Women Never Stop Talking
How Compatible Are You? - Your
 Relationship Quiz Book
Why Men Don't Have A Clue
Why Women Always Need More Shoes!
Talk Language
Get It Write

www.PeaseInternational.com